KEY - Books 6, 6½, 7, 8

Explode The Code

Nancy Hall and Rena Price

Explode The Code, for use in the primary and elementary grades, teaches the basic phonics concepts necessary for beginning through intermediate readers. All the workbooks in the **Explode The Code** series strengthen visual perception by helping students see the differences between various letters and words that are similar. Exercises throughout the lessons present words with letters that students tend to confuse, reverse, or invert.

Included in the program are three primers, **A, B,** and **C**, which introduce the consonant sounds. A three-page Consonant Pretest in **Book 1** measures a student's familiarity with consonant sounds. All books contain a Posttest, which measures a student's overall comprehension of the material covered in the lessons. The Posttests are also effective as pretests. Used as such, a Posttest will help teachers determine where in the program a student should begin. If a Posttest is completed with more than 85 percent accuracy, the material in that book probably would be unnecessary and repetitive. However, a careful evaluation of the student's responses, combined with the teacher's assessment of the student's needs, will help the teacher decide whether parts of the book would be appropriate as review or as remedial work.

The illustrated workbooks in this program all contain a series of eleven to fifteen lessons, each approximately eight pages long. Each lesson follows a consistent format designed to reinforce the phonetic patterns in a sequential manner. Simple directions are included at the top of each workbook page. Only minimal guidance from the teacher should be necessary. When requested to do so, teachers should help students identify pictures. Sight words used in each book are listed on the inside back cover. Teachers should introduce these words as they are needed.

It is suggested that students complete an entire lesson in no more than two sittings, since each lesson teaches one phonetic concept in a variety of ways. Students should be allowed to proceed through the lessons at their own pace, however. Those who have learned cursive writing should be encouraged to use it in the writing exercises.

The **Explode The Code** series consists of **Books A, B, C, 1, 1 ½ 2, 2 ½, 3, 3 ½, 4, 4 ½, 5, 5 ½, 6, 6 ½, 7, and 8.** The workbooks provide teachers and students with an instructive program to supplement classroom materials.

Contents of Books 6, 6½, 7, and 8

Book 6 contains fifteen lessons and a four-page **Posttest. Lesson 1** introduces *ar* words; **Lesson 2**, *or* words; **Lesson 3**, *er, ir, ur*, words; **Lesson 4**, *wor, war* words; **Lesson 5,** review; **Lesson 6** teaches *igh*; **Lesson 7**, sounds of *oo*; **Lesson 8**, *ea*; **Lesson 9**, *ie*; **Lesson 10**, review; **Lesson 11**, diphthongs *oi, -oy*; **Lesson 12**, diphthongs *ou, ow*; **Lesson 13**, *au, aw*; **Lesson 14**, *ew, ui, ue, ou*; **Lesson 15**, review.

Book 6 1/2 provides additional practice on the concepts introduced in Book 6. It contains thirteen lessons and a **Posttest. Lesson 1** presents *ar* words; **Lesson 2**, *or* words; **Lesson 3**, *er, ir, ur*, and *ear* words; **Lesson 4**, *wor* and *war* words; **Lesson 5**, *igh* words; **Lesson 6,** *oo* words; **Lesson 7**, *ea* words; **Lesson 8**, *ie* and *ey* words; **Lesson 9**, *oi* and *oy* words; **Lesson 10**, *ou* and *ow* words; **Lesson 11**, *au* and *aw* words; **Lesson 12**, *ew, ui, ue,* and *ou* words; **Lesson 13**, review.

Book 7 contains fifteen lessons and a four-page **Posttest. Lesson 1** introduces words with *c* followed by *e, i,* or *y*; **Lesson 2**, *g* followed by *e, i* or *y*; **Lesson 3**, *-dge* words; **Lesson 4**, review; **Lesson 5** teaches *-mb* words; **Lesson 6**, *kn-* words; **Lesson 7**, *wr-* words; **Lesson 8**, silent *t* words; **Lesson 9**, silent *h* words; **Lesson 10**, review; **Lesson 11**, *ear* says /air/; **Lesson 12**, *ear* says /er/; **Lesson 13**, *ph* words; **Lesson 14**, words with *ei, eigh*; **Lesson 15**, review.

Book 8 contains thirteen lessons and a four-page **Posttest. Lesson 1** introduces *-ness*, *-less* suffixes; **Lesson 2**, *-ous*, *-or* suffixes; **Lesson 3**, *-ist*, *-ity* suffixes; **Lesson 4** review; **Lesson 5** teaches *-ture*, *-ment*; **Lesson 6**, *-able*, *-ible* words; **Lesson 7**, *-sion*, *-tion*; **Lesson 8**, review; **Lesson 9** introduces *-ance*, *-ence* endings; **Lesson 10**, *-tive*, *-sive*; **Lesson 11**, *-ify*, *-ize* endings; **Lesson 12**, *ti*, *ci* words; **Lesson 13**, review.

Directions for Posttests.

The teacher dictates part of each **Posttest**; the students complete part of it independently. The **Posttests** for each book may be administered to an individual or to a group.

Answers for Book 6

page 121—Students circle the words with the same vowel sound, according to the directions at the top of the page. These words are:

1. frown/couch
2. field/teach
3. blest/spread
4. glide/slight
5. moist/oyster
6. churn/third
7. stoop/flew
8. shows/groans
9. world/churn
10. chain/paste
11. fault/drawn
12. fruit/gloom

page 122—Give the instruction, "Circle the word you hear," and dictate the words listed below. The students circle the correct word from a choice of five words.

1. squirming
2. sprawling
3. powdery
4. chiefly
5. frightening
6. withdrew
7. northeaster
8. pleasant
9. harpooned
10. understood

page 123—Students write sentences dictated by the teacher. Dictate each sentence slowly once or twice. It is often helpful for the students to repeat the sentence before they write it.

1. The stars and the moon shine at night.
2. You can use a straw to sip a milkshake.
3. A storm from the north may blow hard.
4. I can see my footprints in the sawdust.
5. Pork chops smell good when Mom broils them
6. A toothbrush helps to make your mouth clean.

page 124—Students complete this page on their own. Simple directions are included at the top of the Posttest. The students read short paragraphs and select the words that best complete the sentences. These words are:

1. moonlit, surf, foot, shark, beach
2. warning, outdoors, lightning, burning, fireworks
3. worms, sneakers, barefoot, trout, ground, raccoon

Answers for Book 6½

Page 105—Students circle the words with the same vowel sound, according to the directions at the top of the page. These words are:

1. balloon/glue
2. beach/steam
3. cry/flight
4. warmth/storm
5. caught/yawn
6. roast/most
7. count/scout
8. learn/burnt
9. point/boy
10. word/purse
11. thirst/hurt
12. steak/break

Page 106—Give the instruction, "Circle the word you hear," and dictate the words listed below. The students circle the correct word from a choice of five words.

1. unearthed
2. worst
3. heavy
4. fielder
5. rousted
6. threw
7. lightest
8. believe
9. couches
10. sprouted

Page 107—Students write sentences dictated by the teacher. Dictate each sentence slowly once or twice. It is often helpful for the students to repeat the sentence before they try it.

1. The carpenter is pointing to her wooden toolbox.
2. Which person threw the old newspapers out?
3. The outlaw hauled the highchair into the tower.
4. The hockey team met at the field for a workout.
5. How did you learn to count by tens?

Page 108—Students complete this page on their own. Simple directions are included at the top of the Posttest. The students read short paragraphs and select the words that best complete the sentences. These words are:

1. newspaper, break, underneath, auto, looking, outlaws, highway, warning, report
2. jockey, shorter, heavy, pounds, horseback, high, willpower, thousand, worthwhile
3. fireworks, ballfield, pointing, noisy, shower, shouted, backward, brightest, loudest

Copyright © 1999, 1994, 1992, 1990 by Educators Publishing Service, Inc. All rights reserved. No part of this book may be reproduced or utilized in any form or by any electronic or mechanical means, including photocopying, without permission in writing from the publisher. Printed in U.S.A. ISBN 0-8388-1793-9

June 1999 Printing

Answers for Book 7

page 3
2. contest/concert
3. penny/pencil
4. applesauce/apple cider
5. peaceful/forceful
6. replace/recess
7. decide/defeat

page 5
2. circus
3. cider
4. circle
5. decide
6. juicy
7. center

page 7
1. to a fancy ball at the royal palace
2. blue lace
3. twice
4. ice-cream sandwiches and apple cider
5. Her glass slippers were too tight.
6. rock and roll music

page 11
1. package/bandage
2. stingy/spongy
3. gentle/turtle
4. ginger/gerbil
5. vegetable/changeable
6. postage/teenage
7. marble/margin

page 13
1. gentleman
2. postage
3. sponge cake
4. gerbil
5. vegetables
6. changed
7. teenager

page 15
1. orange
2. nothing; She didn't have a bandage.
3. change
4. strange
5. to get an ice-cream cone
6. ginger

page 19
1. gadget/budget
2. mistake/misjudge
3. fruitcake/fudge cake
4. Dodger/badger
5. hammering/sledgehammer
6. handbag/baggage
7. drawstring/drawbridge

page 21
1. smudge
2. gadget
3. judge
4. edging
5. police badge
6. dodge
7. hedge

page 23
1. the rickety bridge
2. an old jeep
3. dizzy
4. between some rocks at the edge of the road
5. a lodge; some help
6. tomorrow

page 27
1. bracelet/embrace
2. dancer/saucer
3. larger/stranger
4. advantage/cottage
5. priceless/helpless
6. princess/recess
7. icing/racing

page 29
1. unlace
2. grocery
3. stranger
4. cottage
5. passenger
6. exchange
7. excellent

page 31
1. advanced
2. advice
3. solar energy
4. furnace
5. success
6. huge/gigantic

page 32—Crossword Puzzle
Across
1. pod
3. city
5. bandage
6. cry
7. east
9. princess
11. gym
12. palace
13. rice
15. giant
16. fudge

Down
1. pray
2. dodges
3. cages
4. yes
5. bracelet
8. tiger
9. plunge
10. sick
12. pea
14. ice

page 35
1. tremble/crumble
2. combing/honeycomb
3. lamb chop/chopsticks
4. bluebell/dumbbell
5. thumbnail/thumbtack
6. nutshell/bombshell
7. excite/recite

page 37
1. plumber
2. climbing
3. lamb chops
4. thumbnail
5. beachcomber
6. combing
7. crumb cake

page 39
1. a comb
2. Paula; the plumber
3. to fix the leaky pipes in the bathroom
4. She had had to climb up.
5. her thumb
6. dumbbell

page 44
1. capsize/kneecap
2. knickknack/knickers
3. jackknife/jacket
4. knockout/knocker
5. knothole/knotted
6. sackful/knapsack
7. sprinkle/knuckle

page 45
1. knapsack
2. knee socks
3. doorknob
4. know-how
5. knitted
6. slipknots
7. jackknife

page 47
1. to protect a huge palace from dragons
2. his knapsack
3. because it's not a good idea (not safe)
4. There were too many knots for him to tie.
5. a knife
6. *Answers will vary.*

page 51
1. voyage/wreckage
2. whisper/wrapper
3. wrinkle/twinkle
4. wristwatch/watchdog
5. shipwreck/shipment
6. handwriting/handkerchief
7. tennis/written

page 53
1. handwriting
2. wrinkled
3. written
4. wrongdoing
5. shipwrecked
6. wrapped
7. wristband

page 55
1. a brand new ten-speed racing bike
2. She flipped a wheelie.
3. Norma's wrist
4. She could not write or do her homework.
5. a hammer and wrench
6. wrinkled

page 59
1. wrestler/whistler
2. listen/hasten
3. often/fasten
4. bristle/gristle
5. soften/glisten
6. sandcastle/sandwich
7. whistle/thistle

page 61
1. bristles
2. hastens
3. often
4. listen
5. whistling
6. rustle
7. wrestled

page 63
1. a haunted castle, surrounded by a deep moat
2. a shrill whistle
3. the Evil Knight
4. the giant key to the drawbridge
5. a large, fierce dog
6. the gold lamp

page 67
1. barber/rhubarb
2. ghostly/hourly
3. glassful/hourglass
4. exhaust/exhibit
5. actor/honor
6. gritty/honesty
7. herbal/general

page 69
1. ghost
2. exhausted
3. herbs
4. honor
5. shepherds
6. honesty

7. hour

page 71
1. Any of the following: He was shy, kind and honorable; he didn't like to scare people; he often felt scared.
2. Oscar the rhino
3. Rhode Island
4. They didn't like anyone who was different.
5. rhubarb and herbs
6. that he can be happy even though he is different

page 75
1. outcast/knock out
2. loophole/knothole
3. honeycomb/honeymoon
4. kneecap/capsize
5. knitted/spotted
6. doorbell/doorknob
7. stagecoach/stagehand

page 77
1. castle
2. wreckage
3. climbing
4. ghostlike
5. knives
6. wallet
7. knee socks

page 79
1. wrapped
2. fasten
3. the hour
4. wrestling
5. scraps
6. climbed

page 80—Crossword Puzzle
Across
1. knight
4. honest
6. juice
7. stage
8. whistle
12. orange
13. magic
14. city
16. wreath
18. knothole
20. lamb
21. wreck
22. badge

Down
2. ice
3. thistle
5. egg
9. honeycomb
10. wristwatch
11. racer

15. ink
16. wrench
17. hour
19. climb

page 83
1. underneath/underwear
2. misshaped/pear-shaped
3. suitable/bearable
4. swearing/wrecking
5. footwear/footstool
6. squirting/tearing
7. billfold/billboard

page 85
1. leaking
2. wash-and-wear
3. Smokey the Bear
4. cream puff
5. underwear
6. seat belt
7. tearing

page 87
1. He wanted to join the navy and see the world.
2. a white sailor suit
3. pear-shaped
4. He tried to raise his arm to salute.
5. to stop eating honey
6. *Answers will vary.*

page 91
1. earthquake/earthworm
2. searchlight/twilight
3. earnings/feelings
4. unearth/unheard
5. learning/searching
6. earthenware/hardware
7. rehearse/repeat

page 93
1. rehearsal
2. earthworms
3. searchlight
4. earliest
5. earthquake
6. earning
7. learn

page 95
1. He was very strong and powerful; he could do almost anything.
2. catch a fish
3. his searchlight
4. an early bird
5. the earth
6. an earthquake

page 99
1. phonograph/photograph
2. telephone/telescope

3. dolphin/dollar
4. paragraph/autograph
5. orphan/orchard
6. phantom/tomahawk
7. better/alphabet

page 101
1. dolphin
2. alphabet
3. phone
4. elephant
5. trophy
6. phantom

page 103
1. star
2. a trophy
3. a dolphin named Phanny
4. a gopher named Go-Go
5. She called them on the telephone.
6. She was big and they were small; it was dangerous.

page 107
1. reindeer/deerskin
2. eighty/eighteen
3. neighborhood/childhood
4. cowbells/sleighbells
5. unveil/unfair
6. overweight/overalls
7. underweight/underground

page 109
1. sleighbells
2. neighborhood
3. eighty-eight
4. weightlessness
5. overweight
6. reindeer
7. eighteen

page 111
1. an athlete
2. twenty-eight
3. at a neighborhood gym
4. eighty pounds
5. all the neighbors
6. Rhoda made the Olympic team. (*Answers may vary.*)

page 115
1. center/centipede
2. earphone/earring
3. attic/gigantic
4. sausage/passage
5. equipment/cement
6. cabbage/garbage
7. spaceship/friendship

page 117
1. billfold
2. overweight
3. writing
4. faucet
5. fierce
6. overheard
7. knives

page 119
1. freckles
2. scratching
3. pencil
4. listened
5. decided
6. thumbnail

page 120—Crossword Puzzle
Across
2. wreck
4. freight
6. advice
8. practice
10. autograph
11. gentleman
12. wrist
13. race
15. wet
16. knotted
17. mice

Down
1. general
3. officer
5. hour
7. honest
8. phone
9. celebrate
11. gentle
14. end

Posttests—These may be administered to an individual or to a group.

page 121
1. crumb
2. shepherd
3. wrist
4. honest
5. palace
6. lamb
7. strange
8. pledge
9. knob
10. listen

page 122
3. December
4. photograph
5. celebrate
6. neighborhood
7. cucumber
8. no word
9. gymnastic
10. gigantic
11. no word
12. messenger

page 123
whistles, thumb, comb, telephone, fence, wrap, climbed, knocked

page 124
1. He was seventy-eight years old, and he ran in a marathon.
2. He jogged ten miles every day.
3. Any of the following: It is important not to run too fast, but to pace oneself; always breathe through your mouth; never look down at the ground.
4. He got more cheers than the winner.

Answers for Book 8

page 4
1. stranger / strangeness
2. polite / politeness
3. noise / noiseless
4. value / valueless
5. slippery / slipperiness
6. gloomy / gloominess
7. reckless / recklessness

page 5
2. kindness
3. careless
4. rudeness
5. weightless
6. emptiness
7. fearless

page 6
1. without/without
2. powerless
3. cloudless
4. the sourness
5. thankfulness
6. dampness
7. blameless

page 9
1. cloudless, dampness, foolishness, wireless, craziness, helpfulness, coolness
2. hot, cloudless, muggy, dampness, humid
3. helpless
4. smartness
5. *Answers will vary.*

page 12
1. conduct / conductor

2. mountain
   mountainous
3. hazard
   hazardous
4. act
   actor
5. invent
   inventor
6. humor
   humorous
7. edit
   editor

page 12
1. nervous
2. governor
3. continuous
4. spectator
5. enormous
6. instructor
7. ridiculous

page 14
person/person
1. an editor
2. generous
3. an advisor
4. an inspector
5. the director
6. glamorous
7. furious

page 17
1. hazardous, fabulous, marvelous, enormous, nervous, spectators, tremendous, furious, ridiculous, curios, hazardous
2. I could not breathe
3. nervous
4. savior
5. Answers will vary

page 20
1. stupid
   stupidity
2. final
   finalists
3. personal
   personality
Note: person is also an acceptable answer.
4. touring
   tourist
5. major
   majority
6. violin
   violinist
7. solo
   soloist

page 21
1. pianist

2. calamity
3. motorist
4. ability
5. violinist
6. security
7. tourist

page 22
person/person
1. a motorist
2. stupidity
3. a novelist
4. a community
5. captivity
6. a necessity
7. a dentist

page 25
1. festivity, druggist, pianist, violinist, flutist, organist, ability, activity, majority, necessity, calamity
2. eat six artichokes
3. calamity
4. ability
5. *Answers will vary*.

page 27
1. professor
   protector
2. curious
   curiosity
3. humorous
   humorless
4. cheerfulness
   cheerless
5. humanity
   humidity
6. generous
   generosity

page 28
1. dangerous
2. gentleness
3. sleeveless
4. director
5. darkness
6. organist
7. poisonous

page 29
1. (3) feeling envy toward another
2. (2) dampness in the air
3. (3) without much thought or planning
4. (2) a sense of being unlived in
5. (3) very loud like thinder
6. (3) one who rides a bike
7. (1) a chance for advancement

page 30
1. studious
2. collector

3. dentist
4. professor
5. blameless
6. curious
7. jealous

page 31
Word Search

```
R E C K L E S S W X
A M N P F A M O U S
X D M Q R S U W V H
Q T Y G B L X O S U
V U B N L B P V M M
P D R U G G I S T I
R B A H I J L S O D
O Q I K L B M Y C I
F R N H G C V V H T
E N L J F D W K I Y
S W E E T N E S S F
S V S W D F G X H K
O S S R Q P L Z J G
R T R O S R K P S S
T R E M E N D O U S
```

reckless   brainless
famous   sweetness
humidity   professor
druggist   tremendous

page 33
1. humorous, curious, fabulous
2. He collected clothespins; or He peeked at toes; or He acted heartbroken.
3. (c) Joe Crow made an interesting and humorous pet.
4. Joe might have been elected governor because everybody loved him./Everybody loved Joe because he was such a fabulous bird.
5. edit, marvel, direct, glamor, humor, visit, poison, collect
6. (a) generous (b) curious (c) collector (d) enormous

page 36
1. moist
   moisture
2. departure
   depart
3. astonishing
   astonishment
4. disappointment
   appointment
5. mixture
   mix
6. prove
   improvement
7. arrange
   arrangement

page 37
1. disagreement

2. advancement
3. imprisonment
4. astonishment
5. moisture
6. puncture
7. basement

page 38

/chur/
1. argument
2. a measurement
3. a puncture
4. an imprisonment
5. a disappointment
6. an apartment
7. a fracture

page 41

1. disagreement, assignment, departure, punishment, arrangement, basement, disappointment, imprisonment, adventure, comment
2. departure note
3. disappointment
4. punishment
5. Answers will vary.

page 44

1. valueless
   valuable
2. favored
   unfavorable
3. combust
   combustible
4. depend
   dependable
5. presented
   presentable
6. divide
   divisible
7. wash
   washable

page 45

1. excitable
2. sensible
3. valuable
4. miserable
5. possible
6. uncomfortable
7. usable

page 46

able/able
1. horrible
2. changeable
3. responsible
4. adorable
5. usable
6. excitable
7. breakable

page 49

1. unforgettable, favorable, invisible, incredible, changeable, possible, miserable, visible, terrible, unmistakable
2. The weather report that morning was favorable.
3. unmistakable
4. sensible
5. Answers will vary.

page 52

1. add
   addition
2. instructor
   instructions
3. elect
   elections
4. express
   expression
5. televise
   television
6. starve
   starvation
7. motion
   motionless

page 53

1. celebration
2. starvation
3. erosion
4. relaxation
5. medication
6. exploration
7. separation

page 54

/shun/
1. medication
2. satisfaction
3. a donation
4. a promotion
5. a solution
6. an operation
7. transportation

page 57

1. expedition, location, instruction, explorations, occasion, permission, motion, attention, illusion
2. strange happenings/moon was full/scary explorations/late at night/trees were shivering/dark park/silver and strange/long walk/shadowy stillness
3. attention
4. occasion
5. Answers will vary.

page 59

1. protection
   protector
2. collector
   collection
3. nature
   naturalist
4. instructions
   instructor
5. visible
   invisible
6. invention
   infections

page 60

subtraction
1. suitable
2. adoption
3. moisture
4. digestion
5. improvement
6. trainable
7. entertainment

page 61

1. (2) something unreal or imagined
2. (3) a time that is to come
3. (3) a mimic or one who copies another
4. (2) fit or safe to eat
5. (1) proper; well-suited
6. (3) having become dirty or poisonous
7. (3) makes

page 62

1. adorable
2. connection
3. future
4. captivity
5. equipment
6. occasion
7. amazement

page 63

Word Search

```
M I N F O R M A T I O N S T
H M A T I O C L M S P O R V
U P T O W N A D O R A B L E
M O I S T U R E X P U L S X
O S O C H E E R T I C A G P
R E I L P U L Y C G K O S L
W B A M A Z E M E N T F J O
M E N T N R S V Z P H L D S
Q T I M P O S S I B L E X I
B G K S O W A Q Y I U M E O
W C A Q G M U K I O Y S E N
```

careless   humor
explosion   adorable
moisture   amazement
impossible   information

page 65

1. adventure, unbelievable,

enjoyable, occasion
2. Lighted propane torches force heat into the balloon by a fan.
3. (a) security (b) alertness (c) collision (d) calamity (e) community
4. A balloonist puts more hot air into the balloon to make it rise (to keep it from crashing into the trees)./ The wind controls the direction and speed of a balloon.
5. son *or* person *or* personal
   loon *or* ball *or* balloon
   fest
   major
   tour
   maze *or* amaze
   alert
   noise *or* noiseless
6. (d) Ballooning is an exciting activity.

page 68
1. prefer
   preference
2. assist
   assistance
3. reappear
   disappearance
4. interfere
   interference
5. annoying
   annoyance
6. acquainted
   acquaintance
7. allowable
   allowance

page 69
1. silence
2. abundance
3. intelligence
4. elegance
5. disappearance
6. commence
7. annoyance

page 70
dance/fence
1. disappearance
2. a disturbance
3. obedience
4. your audience
5. the evidence
6. an annoyance
7. have endurance

page 73
1. difference, audience, guidance, difference, obedience, tolerance, annoyance, disturbance, evidence
2. jump on laps and couches/nibble at ears and rugs/give kisses/nudge elbows
3. obedience
4. guidance
5. *Answers will vary.*

page 76
1. expense
   expensive
2. collection
   recollect
3. captive
   captivity
4. actor
   inactive
5. expression
   expressive
6. impressive
   impression
7. produce
   productive

page 77
1. native
2. massive
3. detective
4. decorative
5. expensive
6. secretive
7. creative

page 78
1. massive
2. negative
3. attentive
4. creative
5. decorative
6. inactive
7. talkative

page 81
1. detectives, extensive, attractive, captive, massive, decorative, impressive, attentive, disruptive
2. secluded/extensive reefs
3. disruptive
4. active
5. *Answers will vary.*

page 84
1. visual
   visualize
2. simple
   simplify
3. realize
   realization
4. motorist
   motorized
5. critic
   criticize
6. note
   notify
7. apology
   apologize

page 85
/if-i/ or /i-fi/
1. electrify
2. apologize
3. magnify
4. memorize
5. simplify
6. identify
7. qualify

page 86
1. apologize
2. hypnotize them
3. memorize it
4. recognize him
5. modernize it
6. beautify it
7. liquefy it

page 89
1. organized, hypnotize, realized, recognize, identify, visualize
2. hypnotize people and turn them into bears
3. visualize
4. recognize
5. *Answers will vary.*

page 92
1. office
   official
2. music
   musician
3. finances
   financial
4. caution
   cautious
5. politics
   politician
6. electric
   electrician
7. part
   partial

page 93
1. suspicious
2. essential
3. artificial
4. delicious
5. repetitious
6. financial
7. patient

page 94
1. delicious
2. suspicious
3. special
4. essential

5. a musician
6. cautious
7. an official

page 97
1. Martian, special, Martian, essential, suspicious, cautiously, luscious, patient, delicious, unofficial, social

Note: For *ti* or *ci* to say /sh/, there must be a vowel following it. Thus in *decided* it does not say /sh/.
2. suspicious
3. social
4. repetitious
5. *Answers will vary.*

page 99
1. questions
   questionable
2. illustrator
   illustrations
3. presents
   representative
4. dependable
   independence
5. patient
   patience
6. information
   informative

page 100
1. capitalize
2. equalize
3. flexible
4. allowance
5. violinist
6. courageous
7. performance

page 101
1. (1) eager for advancement
2. (3) surroundings
3. (3) able to be thrown away after using
4. (2) a movement or motion of one's hands or body
5. (3) excessively active
6. (1) helpful
7. (1) liquid turning into vapor

page 102
1. florist
2. relatives
3. desirables
4. nonreturnable
5. immovable
6. reliable
7. impatient

page 103
Word Search

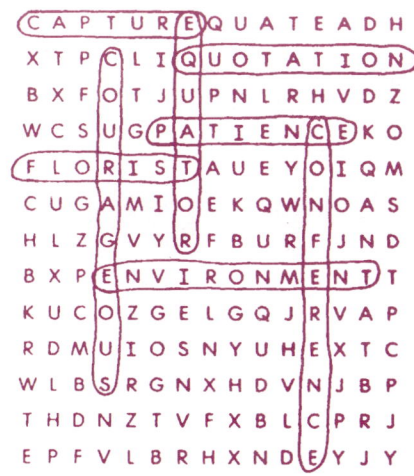

capture
florist
equator
patience
quotation
conference
courageous
environment

page 105
1. reliable, essential, valuable
2. Driving on the dunes destroys the environment.
3. (a) impatient (b) immovable (c) relatives (d) gestured (e) cautious
4. You let some air out of a jeep's tires before going out on the beach./ We had unexpected trouble at Race Point because the sand was fine, and we went too close to the water.
5. *quest* or *question*
   pen or *depend*
   talk
   sport, *port* or *transport*
   direct
   fort or *comfort*
   perfect
   rage or *courage*
6. (c) Think and use caution on any kind of adventure.

Posttests—Posttests may be administered to an individual or to a group.

page 106—Visual Discrimination
acquainted—acquaintance
dexterous—dexterity
fortify—fortification
defective—defection
investigator—investigation
hazardous—hazard
destructive—indestructible
production—reproductive
patience—impatient
dependent—independence
hyperactive—activity
collective—recollection

page 107
1. tial/essential—necessary
2. ment/improvement—advancement
3. cious/luscious—delicious
4. ity/festivity—celebration
5. sive/expensive—costly
6. ance/annoyance—bother
7. ous/fabulous—marvelous

1. tious/cautious—reckless
2. tive/attractive—horrible
3. ity/captivity—freedom
4. tive/hyperactive—inactive
5. ment/disagreement—understanding
6. cious/suspicious—trustful
7. ment/punishment—reward

page 108
1. active
2. abundance
3. essential
4. imitator
5. pollution
6. flexible
7. prosperous

page 109
1. observation
2. reservation
3. starvation
4. conservation

1. oppressive
2. impressive
3. expressive

1. reference
2. difference
3. preference
4. indifference
5. interference

Educators Publishing Service, Inc.
31 Smith Place
Cambridge, MA 02138
1-800-225-5750   www.epsbooks.com

ISBN 0-8388-1793-9

9 780838 817933